THE STORY OF YOUR HAND

THE STORY OF YOUR HAND

by Dr. Alvin Silverstein
and Virginia B. Silverstein

illustrated by Greg Wenzel

G. P. PUTNAM'S SONS   NEW YORK

For Linda Babeu

Library of Congress Cataloging in Publication Data
Silverstein, Alvin.
    The story of your hand.
    Summary: Describes the anatomy of the hand and
discusses the many things hands can do, how left- or
right-handedness is developed, and how gestures are
used in communication.
    1. Hand—Anatomy—Juvenile literature. 2. Hand—
Juvenile literature. 3. Left and right-handedness—
Juvenile literature. 4. Gesture—Juvenile literature.
[1. Hand. 2. Left- and right-handedness. 3. Gesture]
I. Silverstein, Virginia B. II. Title.
QM548.S47 1985   611'.97   85-520
ISBN 0-399-61212-2

Contents

1 / Amazing Hands   7

2 / Hands: The Outside Story   14

3 / Hands: The Inside Story   35

4 / Left Hand, Right Hand   55

5 / Let Your Fingers Do the Talking   66

Index   77

1 / Amazing Hands

There's a squirrel sitting in an oak tree across from our window. It's perched on a branch, eating an acorn. It holds the nut clasped firmly in its two front paws while it nibbles, turning the acorn from time to time to reach the last bits of tasty nutmeat. How cute, we think. It's holding the acorn in its hands, just like a little person.

It isn't, really. There are some important differences between a squirrel's "hands" and the way it uses them, and the true hands of a human being. A squirrel uses its front paws for holding objects like acorns, but when it wants to grasp or carry something it must use its mouth. For holding an object it uses a two-handed grip. It could not hold anything in just one "hand" the way a person can do with ease.

The big difference is the thumb. A squirrel's thumbs are just short little stubs, not good for much. It grasps things with the four "fingers" of each front paw. A human hand—your own hand, for example—is quite different. There are four long fingers at the end of the hand, arranged roughly parallel to each other like the "fingers" of a squirrel's paw. But the thumb that sticks out at an angle from the side of the hand is sturdy and strong and can move around freely. It is what scientists call an *opposable* thumb: you can move your thumb and fingers so that the fleshy pad on the inside of the thumb is exactly opposite the pads at the tip of each finger in turn. Try having someone strap your thumbs tightly to the sides of your hands with adhesive tape, and you'll find out just what it feels like to have "squirrel hands." You can still pick things up by curling your fingers around them, but you'll be rather clumsy. Using two hands, as a squirrel does, gives a little more control. If you take off the tape and free your thumbs, everything will be so much easier!

The amazing human hand can split a block of wood with a karate blow and pick up an egg without crushing it. Hands can wield a hammer to knock in a nail; carry a bucket of water; screw in a light bulb; catch a ball; type on a typewriter; thread a needle; draw pictures; and perform delicate microsurgery on a single living cell, too small to be seen with the naked eye. Capable of crude force or fine control and an incredible variety of movement, hands are all-purpose tools. Their uses seem to be limited only by our imagination.

If you ask a group of biologists what single feature sets humans apart from the other animals, most of them will probably say it is the brain. But some may vote for the hand, or for the upright posture that frees the hands for manipulation. Some animals that walk on four legs do use their forepaws for manipulation. A squirrel holds a nut or berry in its forepaws to eat it. A cat plays

8

with a cornered mouse, giving it gentle taps with a forepaw. A sea otter floats on its back in the water, balancing a flat stone on its chest, and holds a clam in its forepaws, bringing it crashing down on the stone to crack the shell. All these animals use their forepaws as manipulators, but only to a limited degree. The forepaws can be only part-time hands, because their main job is locomotion—moving around from place to place.

Even our closest relatives, the monkeys and apes, use their hands for locomotion. Monkeys grasp branches with their hands and feet as they swing through the trees. They have what might be called "foot-hands." Their long, nimble fingers and thumbs are good for manipulation, but they also have thick, cushiony palm pads that extend back to the wrist, forming a sort of "heel." They walk with all four foot-hands flat on the ground. The apes have true hands, without the footlike heel. But they too use their hands for locomotion. Orangutans, chimpanzees and gorillas all have long arms and long-palmed, long-fingered hands, good for swinging through the trees. On the ground they walk flatfooted on their hind legs, but they cannot walk upright on two feet for more than a few steps. Usually they support part of their weight on the knuckles of their hands. (Hard calluses of thick skin form over the knuckles to protect them.) Apes can use their hands (and feet) for manipulation, and they can even use tools. Biologist Jane Goodall has watched wild chimpanzees gathering and shaping thin sticks to use in fishing termites out of cracks. Chimpanzees raised by humans can be taught to ride bicycles, paint pictures, open locks with a key, and use a variety of other devices designed for human hands. An

monkey's hand

chimpanzee's hand

ape can hold an object between thumb and fingers, but its short thumb and long fingers make the grip rather inefficient. A chimpanzee is more likely to pick things up by curling its fingers around them. A gorilla's hand is closer to the human shape, with the longest thumb and shortest fingers of all the great apes.

A few million years ago, apelike creatures who could walk upright appeared on the earth. Their brains were larger than those of their ape relatives, and their hands no longer had to do double duty as feet. They could pick up and manipulate things even while they were walking around, and they could carry things from place to place. This was an important advantage. It meant that they could gather food and carry it back to their homes—more food than they could carry clenched in their jaws. They could take tools and weapons along with them. And they could carry their babies around securely, safe in the grasp of a hand. These apelike creatures flourished and multiplied. Among their descendants, those with the largest brains and the best ideas about how to use their hands were the most likely to survive. At last true humans appeared.

We humans still show some traces of our monkey and ape ancestry. A human baby crawls with the palms of its hands flat on the floor, just like the foot-hands of a monkey. We can support ourselves by our arms while climbing a rope ladder or swinging from the rings or parallel bars in a gym. And we even use the knuckle-walking posture sometimes—not to walk, but to support ourselves, for example, when standing at a table, giving a speech.

Take a moment to think about all the things you have done since

you got up this morning. Most of them—perhaps all of them—
involved the use of your hands. You reached out a hand to turn off
the alarm clock; you used your hands to pull on your clothes and
fasten buttons and zippers, to turn the water faucets on and off and

guide the toothbrush that cleaned your teeth, to pick up a piece of toast or raise a glass of milk or a spoonful of cereal to your mouth. All through the day you were using your hands constantly. Even now, as you are reading this book, your eyes are moving back and forth along the lines of print, but your hands are turning the pages.

In thinking about all the things your hands have done for you today, you probably missed two kinds of activities. In addition, to using tools and acting as tools themselves, hands are an important part of the way we communicate. We do most of our communicating with words, but we can also say a great deal with gestures. Hand gestures can be very expressive. Some are purposeful and formal, like the hand signals you use when you ride a bike. The hand gestures we use when we speak are often made unconsciously, but they can make our words more interesting and colorful. Even little unconscious habits like folding the hands and drumming on a tabletop can give clues about a person's state of mind.

Hands are also sense organs, the major organs of our sense of touch. They can bring us information about the world, and then—unlike our eyes or ears—they are in a good position to do something about the new information. In the chapters that follow, we'll find out more about the story of the hand—what it is and how it works as a manipulator, a communicator, and an information gatherer.

2 / Hands: The Outside Story

Take a good look at the hands on the next dozen people you see; you'll find that hands come in a variety of sizes, shapes and colors. Some are pale (though living hands are never "lily white"), some are dark, and some are dotted with freckles or "liver spots." Some hands look smooth; others are rough or wrinkled or hairy. Some people have broad hands with short, thick fingers; others have narrow hands with long, slender fingers.

Have you ever tried to guess a person's occupation from the appearance of his or her hands? Tough calluses on the fingertips and palms suggest a job involving hard physical labor, such as building houses or roads. A person with very long fingernails probably *doesn't* work as a typist or play a musical instrument such as a guitar. People tend to think of certain types of hand as suitable for particular professions. Long, slender hands are thought to be necessary for surgeons, who must do delicate cutting and stitching, and for pianists, who must reach notes up and down the keyboard. Yet there are exceptions: some of the most skillful and famous surgeons have broad, square-shaped hands that seem better suited to a construction worker; and one of the most talented classical pianists, Alicia de Larrocha, has very small, short-fingered hands.

With all their variety, human hands do have some basic features in common. The five-digit design passed down from distant mammal ancestors has become four fingers and an opposable thumb. Occasionally people are born with six fingers, or even more, on a hand. The English queen Ann Boleyn, second wife of Henry VIII, had six fingers on one of her hands. Portraits generally show her with that hand in a pocket or partly hidden in a fold of her dress. (In those days, a six-fingered hand was thought to be a sign of a witch.) Possessing more than the normal five digits on a hand is referred to as *polydactyly*. Another fairly rare variation of finger structure is *syndactyly*, in which two fingers are connected by a flap of skin between them, like the webs on a duck's feet. These variations occur in perhaps one in a thousand people. Another kind of variation, *ectrodactyly*, refers to missing fingers. Ectrodactyly is rare in real people, but cartoonists often draw hands as though they had only three or four digits instead of five. Hands are very difficult to draw realistically, and in the quick sketch of a cartoon a hand with

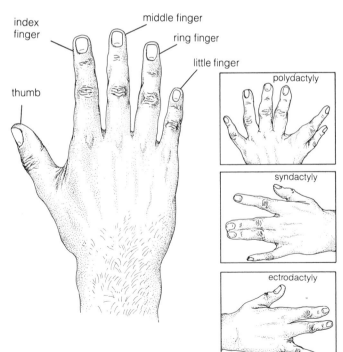

index finger

middle finger

ring finger

little finger

thumb

polydactyly

syndactyly

ectrodactyly

fewer fingers looks better—if you don't examine it too closely.

There is some disagreement about what to call the fingers (five fingers or four fingers and a thumb?) and how they should be numbered. (When you count on your fingers, with which one do you start?) In fact, doctors, lawyers and insurance companies have had so many conflicting ideas about what to call the digits on a hand that each of the fifty states in the United States has enacted legislation establishing standards for them. Unfortunately, there are about ten different systems of "standards" in use. Perhaps the safest system is to forget about numbers and use the common names for each digit. Starting from the *thumb*, the next digit is the *index finger* (also called the forefinger); that is the finger typically used for pointing. Then comes the *middle finger*, the longest finger on the hand. (Curiously, one of the synonyms scientists use for this digit is *obscenus*, which comes from the fact that in many cultures an extended middle finger is a rude and insulting gesture.) The next digit is the *ring finger*. It was once rather fancifully believed that the ring finger had a direct connection with the heart. More likely, people prefer to wear rings on this finger because it is the one that moves around the least and thus is least likely to lose a ring. The last of the digits is the *little finger*. Its synonym, "pinkie," probably comes from a Dutch word for the little finger, *pinkje*.

On the average, the width of a human hand is a little less than half its length, and the middle finger is about half the length of the whole hand. In most people the ring finger is longer than the index finger, but in about 22 percent of men and 45 percent of women the index finger is longer. (If you belong to the minority, don't

16

worry about it—the length of the index finger doesn't make any difference in how skillful the hand is.) Next in size comes the little finger, and the thumb is the shortest of all the digits.

The hands are covered by a flexible coat of skin, except for the upper surfaces of the fingertips, which are protected by tough, horny, oval-shaped fingernails. If you look at the skin on your own hands, you will find that it fits rather loosely. You can pinch up a flap of loose skin from the back of your hand, and the skin of the knuckles bulges up in wrinkles and creases when you hold your fingers out straight. But when you bend your fingers and form a fist, the skin tightens and smoothly covers your knuckles. Looking at the under surface of your hand—the palm side—you will see the skin on your fingers bunch up and form deep creases as you close your hand. The crease lines on the inside of the knuckles remain when you straighten your fingers, although the skin tightens up. There are crease lines on the palm, where the skin forms folds as you close your hand. The fit of the skin thus allows for bending, straightening, and all the other movements of the fingers and hand.

Everyone has creases, or *flexure lines*, on the fingers and palms, but there is a great deal of variation in their arrangement. In fact, you will find that the patterns of flexure lines on your own two hands do not match exactly. There is no scientific basis for *palmistry* (telling fortunes from the lines in the palm), except in a very limited sense: certain types of patterns often occur along with particular birth defects or diseases. But palmistry is a very ancient art. It is mentioned in the Bible, and the Roman general Julius

17

Caesar prided himself on his skill as a palm reader. Even today, many people believe that the story of a person's life—even the future—can be read from the lines in the palm. Palmists have names for the major lines. The horizontal line that runs across from the little-finger side of the palm is the heart line. It is supposed to relate to the health of the heart and also to emotional matters including love affairs, marriages and children. The other major horizontal line, which starts on the thumb side of the palm, is the head line. The nature of this line is supposed to indicate whether the person is practical, straightforward, cautious, timid, inconsistent, gloomy, strong in leadership, talented in science or business, imaginative, and so forth. The vertical line that runs around the thumb is the life line. (Most people have comfortingly long life lines.) And the next vertical line out from the thumb is the fate line. Breaks in the lines and the way they merge or cross one another supposedly give further information, and minor creases may signal important life events.

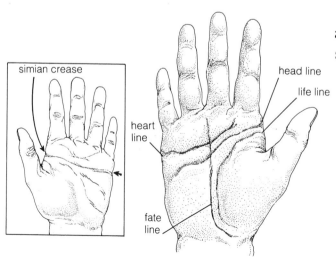

simian crease

heart line

fate line

head line

life line

Actually, the lines in the palm are just hinges along which the skin folds when the fingers are moved. You can see the life line and fate line deepen when you move your thumb in toward the palm, and the heart line and head line deepen when you bend your fingers. In most people the head line and heart line are separate, with a gap between them near the index finger. But a small minority have what is called a *simian crease*: a single horizontal line that runs straight across the palm from one side to the other. Our ape and monkey relatives all have hands with a simian crease. The reason for the difference is that in human hands the index finger has a great deal of independence in its movements, while in monkeys and apes this finger tends to work together with the others. Doctors have found that people born with a type of mental retardation called *Down's syndrome* typically have palms with a simian crease. It may also occur in babies born with heart problems and in those whose mothers suffered from rubella (German measles) during pregnancy.

If you look at your hand with a magnifying glass, the fine crisscrossing creases become much clearer. In addition, you'll notice that the skin of the palm and the fingers is covered with patterns of very fine parallel lines. These are formed by tiny ridges or thickenings in the skin, and they look like a freshly plowed field or a piece of corduroy. Some of the ridges, called *papillary ridges*, run straight; others are curved or even looped into complex patterns. The fingertips of each person have a unique set of patterns of papillary ridges, possessed by no one else in the world (except, perhaps, an identical twin). Each fingertip has a different pattern; even the corresponding fingertips on a person's left and right hands do not match. The patterns can be transferred to paper in the form of *fingerprints* by inking the fingers and then pressing them down one by one. The skin's natural oils and salts also leave traces on everything the fingers touch. These are usually

whorl

loop

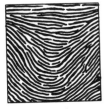

arch

invisible, but they can be made to stand out by treating the surface with fine powder or a chemical. The police use fingerprints left at the scene of a crime to identify criminals. The FBI currently has fingerprints of nearly 200 million men and women on file and identifies the prints of some 40,000 crime suspects each year. Most of the fingerprints on file don't belong to criminals; people may be fingerprinted for identification purposes—on the job, in a hospital, or in school.

Even with modern computers, the idea of sorting through 200 million sets of fingerprints—all different—to see if any of them match seems staggering. Actually, although no two sets are exactly alike, fingerprints do fall into several general patterns. The papillary ridges on the fingertips may form arches, loops or whorls. Large numbers of whorls are often found among Chinese, Japanese and other Far Eastern peoples, while loops are the most common fingerprint pattern among Americans. Women tend to have more arches than men, although you can't tell a person's sex from fingerprints. In addition to the general shapes, prints can be matched according to the number and thickness of papillary ridges (men's ridges are usually thicker than women's) and even the arrangement of the tiny sweat pores. In one criminal case, for example, a thief left a print of his left middle finger on a rosewood box. When they compared a suspect's fingerprint with this clue from the scene of the crime, police experts found more than 900 similarities.

The papillary ridges on the fingers and palms aren't just decorations, or handy devices for catching crooks. They have several useful functions. First of all, like the treads on an automobile tire, they help to increase traction and improve the hand's grip. In addition, the papillary ridges contain tiny fingerlike structures that are linked to the system for sensing touch and pressure. They also contain sweat pores, openings too small to be seen without a magnifier. On the fingertips there may be as many as eighteen sweat pores in a millimeter of papillary ridge. Drops of moisture ooze out from these pores, cause the papillary ridges to swell, and help to improve the grip. (A little bit of moisture helps you hold things better, but when the hands get very wet they are slippery and do not grip well.)

Skin has been described as the structure that keeps the blood in and the rain out. But it is much more than just a waterproof coat. It is a rather complicated structure that does many varied jobs for the body. Skin is a many-layered structure. The outermost layer, the part that we see, is actually dead! It is made up of dead bodies of cells, an average of twenty deep, that have become flattened, tough and horny. This layer of skin is called the *corneal layer*, from a word that means "horny." The horny texture comes from a protein called *keratin*, which also forms the substance of hair and nails. The dead cells of the corneal layer protect the delicate living cells from injury, from drying out, and from attacks by germs and harmful chemicals. Under this outer layer lie three layers of living cells; together with the corneal layer, they make up the *epidermis*, the outer coat of the skin. It is a special kind of coat; it is self-repairing and self-renewing. Each time you wash your hands, you rub off thousands of dead skin cells. Others flake off invisibly as you go through the day. Even at night, when you are sleeping, you are losing skin cells. But new cells are continually being formed to replace them.

An epidermal cell has a life of about four weeks. It starts out at the bottom of the epidermis, as a soft, slim column of living matter. (Most new skin cells are formed in the middle of the night, while you are sleeping quietly and the body's energies are not needed for other activities.) The cell moves upward through the layers, gradually flattening out until it is shaped like a flat paving stone. It produces keratin, and eventually it dies and takes its place in the corneal layer. The dead cell continues to move upward as new cells are formed underneath it and older cells are lost from the outer surface of the skin. Finally it too reaches the surface, and then, in a scratch or a rub, it is gone.

Cross sections of skin

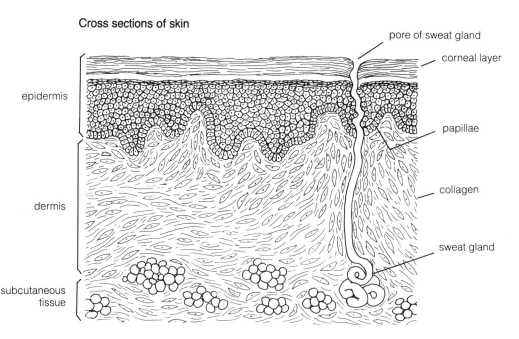

Some of the epidermal cells produce a brown substance called *melanin*. Melanin acts as a sort of natural shield that protects the body tissues from the damaging ultraviolet rays of the sun. Melanin gives a brown color to the skin. The more melanin skin cells produce, the darker the skin will be. Pale skin has very little melanin. Freckles are small areas of skin that produce more melanin than the neighboring cells. (The number of freckles on the hands tends to increase as a person gets older, and they may be called "aging spots.") When skin is exposed to sunlight, the cells make more melanin and you get a suntan. But heredity determines how much melanin the skin cells can produce; the skin of some people is dark even if they have not been in the sun, while others cannot get much of a suntan even if they spend a lot of time outdoors. (People whose skin cells cannot produce much melanin may get a painful sunburn if they spend too much time in the sun.)

Underneath the epidermis lies the true skin, the *dermis*. Its upper layer contains tiny fingerlike *papillae*, which poke up into the epidermis. (Remember the papillary ridges on the fingertips and palms?) The papillae hold nerve endings that carry sense messages and tiny blood vessels that bring nourishing blood to the skin. The lower layer of the dermis is crisscrossed by a dense mat of fibers that give the skin strength and resilience. Most of the fibers are made of a tough, strong protein called *collagen*, but there are also elastic fibers that help to make skin "stretchy." (Try pinching up a bit of loose skin from the back of your hand. As soon as you let go, it will snap right back into place.)

The dermis contains a variety of structures, including sweat glands, hair follicles, oil-producing sebaceous glands, and various specialized sense receptors that gather information about the world around us.

We have already mentioned the numerous tiny sweat pores in the skin of the hands. There are about 220,000 sweat pores in a square inch of skin on the palm. Sweating is an important part of the body's temperature-control system. Watery sweat gathers in the small coiled tubes of the sweat glands and passes out to the surface through sweat pores, carrying some of the body's excess heat along with it. When the temperature goes up, or if you are running or doing some other physical activity that generates a lot of heat, more sweat is produced. Strong emotions such as fear also can make the sweat glands in certain parts of the body work overtime. The sweat glands in the palms of the hands are very sensitive to emotions. Have you ever noticed that when you are nervous your hands get sweaty? That can be embarrassing if you are holding hands with someone you like, or if you meet someone important and have to shake hands. Old-time FBI agents tell a story about their former boss, J. Edgar Hoover. Hoover thought that his men should be calm and in control at all times, and he was very angry if any of the agents showed his nervousness with a sweaty handshake. So the agents were careful to carry around a handkerchief to give their hands a quick wipe if they happened to meet the boss in the hall.

Our mammal ancestors had a thick fur coat over most of the body. We humans have a fur coat, too, but most of our hairs are short and thin. If you look carefully at your hand (you may need to use a magnifier), you will find that you have hair over the back of it and the lower part of the fingers. But the rest of the fingers and the palms are bare. Imagine how difficult it would be to grip something if you had a coat of slippery hair on your palms! Hairs would also interfere with the delicate sense of touch on the fingertips. But the hairs on the back of the hands do play a role in our sense of touch. Tiny nerves wrapped around the root of each hair are stimulated if something makes the hair move. Try running a finger very lightly just above the back of your hand, close but not actually touching the skin. You'll notice an eerie tickly feeling. The hairs on the hands, like those on the rest of the body, are an early-warning system. If a mosquito comes in for a landing, for example, it may brush against a few hairs; then you will feel it before it has a chance to bite.

We think of the hands as our main organs of touch, but actually they have many senses. Various kinds of *sense receptors* in the skin, from simple threadlike nerve endings to more complicated structures, gather information about touch, pressure, pain and temperature. When they are stimulated they send a message to the brain, and we "feel." You can draw a map of your skin senses. First, on the back of your hand, with a washable fiber-tip pen, draw a two-inch grid, ruled into quarter-inch squares. Draw a similar grid on your palm and, for comparison, one on your forearm. On a sheet of paper, draw three grids just like the ones on your skin and label them "back of hand," "palm" and "forearm." Now take a straight pin and touch the flat head lightly to each small box in the grids on your skin in turn. Each time you feel something, make a dot with colored pencil or ink in the corresponding box on the paper. When

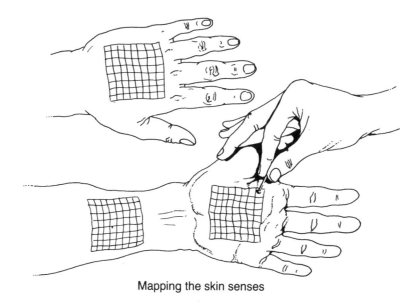

Mapping the skin senses

you finish, you will have color maps of your touch receptors. Next press each box on your skin firmly with the pinhead and enter the results on the paper with dots of a different color. That color will be a map of pressure receptors. Now turn the pin around and press each box with the sharp point of the pin (just hard enough to make an impression, not to break the skin). Use a different color for this map of your pain sense. Now straighten out a paper clip and hold the tip against an ice cube, then press it against a box on the grid. If you can feel a cold sensation, mark the grid on the paper with a new color. Remember to chill the paper clip again each time as you check each box. After you finish mapping your cold receptors, dip the end of the paper clip into a cup of hot water to test for your heat sense, and map that on the paper too.

When you have finished your color maps of the skin senses, compare the patterns of the different-colored dots. Are there more of one type than another? Which are closest together? Are the sense maps different on the hand and the forearm?

The skin of the hands—especially on the fingertips—has the most sensitive sense of touch in the body. In fact, if you tried to draw a map showing the locations of the individual sense receptors on any of the fingertips, even with the finest pin point, quarter-inch-square boxes would show a solid mass of dots, with no blank space at all. There are some other interesting ways to demonstrate how sensitive the fingertips are. Close your eyes and have a friend touch the skin of your fingertip with the points of two well-sharpened pencils, about an inch apart. You will be able to feel the two separate touches distinctly. Now, still keeping your eyes closed, have the friend touch you with the pencil points again, moving them closer this time. Repeat the test, each time moving the points closer, until you can feel only one touch even though both pencil points are in contact with your fingertip. Open your eyes and measure the distance between the two pencil points. Then repeat the same test on the skin of your forearm. Even at an inch apart, you may not be able to tell that there are two separate touches. Another way to demonstrate the touch sensitivity of the hand is to take a hairpin, bent so that the tips are about an inch apart, and run it lightly down the skin of your forearm, past the wrist, and down the skin of your palm. Although two points are touching you at all times, what you *feel* is a single touch that mysteriously branches into two separate touches on your palm.

Although the skin of the hands is extremely sensitive to touch, it is *less* sensitive to temperature than other parts of the body. That is why your hands may feel perfectly comfortable without gloves on a chilly fall day when you need to wear a heavy sweater or jacket. A parent who is warming up a bottle of milk for a baby typically tests a drop of liquid on the wrist, not the finger, to see if it is "body temperature." And you feel a person's forehead for fever with the lips, rather than the hands.

There are some other curious things about the temperature sense. Have you ever noticed that if you touch an ice cube or the inside of the freezer, it seems "burning hot"? That is because the skin has receptors for sensations of cold and warmth, but none for very hot temperatures. Very hot temperatures stimulate a combination of cold and pain senses, producing a warning signal that tells you to do something right away to avoid a dangerous burn. Very cold temperatures also stimulate the pain receptors, so they can easily be confused with the "hot" sensation. Another interesting thing about the skin's temperature sense is that it responds to *changes* in temperature. Place one hand in a bowl of hot water and the other hand in a bowl of cold water. After a few minutes, you will find that both hands are starting to feel comfortable, even though one felt too hot at first and the other felt too cold. Now transfer both hands to a bowl of lukewarm water. Instead of feeling just pleasantly warm, the water will feel hot to the hand that was in cold water and cold to the hand that was in hot water.

Some years ago there were reports that a Russian woman could "see" and even read the print of a newspaper with the skin of her

28

fingertips. Most scientists now believe that her amazing demonstrations were really faked and that she was peeking around the blindfold on her eyes. But the hands can give us an amazing amount of information about the world around us. By touch you can readily distinguish hard metal from soft rubber, or tell the difference between the textures of velvet, cotton and nylon. Handling an object with your eyes closed, you can get a pretty good idea of its size and shape. Try sorting out a handful of mixed change by feel. It's easy to recognize most of the coins, although dimes and pennies may give you a little trouble.

Both the hair and the nails are mostly *keratin*, a protein formed by epidermal cells. You don't bleed or feel pain when you cut your hair or file your nails, because they don't contain any living cells. Hairs are cylinders made of three layers of keratin. The outermost layer forms tiny overlapping scales, which you can see if you look at a hair under a microscope. The color of hair is produced by melanin. Each hair grows in a *follicle*, a sheath of living epidermal cells that tunnel down into the dermis.

The bottom of the follicle is widened and rounded like the bulb of an onion and contains the root of the hair. When you pull a hair out by the roots, that does hurt, because the root is alive. Each hair grows for a while, then stops. After a time the bulb dies, comes loose from the follicle, and the hair falls

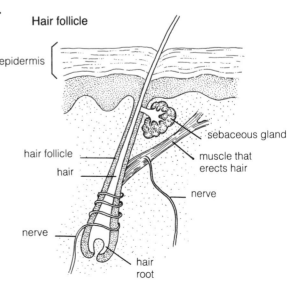

Hair follicle

epidermis

sebaceous gland

hair follicle

muscle that
erects hair

hair

nerve

nerve

hair
root

out. Then a new hair grows out from the bottom of the follicle. Hair grows at different rates at different ages and on different parts of the body. The hair on the head can reach a length of about five feet, but the hairs on the hands grow more slowly and are replaced after a much shorter time, so they are usually only a fraction of an inch long. Hair grows only on the backs of the hands and fingers; on the fingers it grows in small patches. If you look at your own hands, you will find that all the hair is growing in one direction: toward the little-finger side of the hand.

Fingernails are broad plates of transparent, horny keratin that protect the upper surface of the fingertips. Like hairs, a nail has a living root, which is hidden under the skin at the base of the nail. It grows out over the *nail bed*, a plate of living tissue with a rich blood supply. The pink color of fingernails comes from the blood showing through. (If a fingertip is badly bruised, blood vessels in the nail bed may be damaged and may bleed. The blood clots that form make a part of the nail look black.) If you lose your whole nail in an accident, it can still grow back as long as the root is undamaged. At the base of each nail, air pockets form a half-moon-shaped area

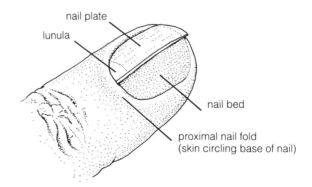

nail plate

lunula

nail bed

proximal nail fold
(skin circling base of nail)

called the *lunula*. (Its name means "little moon.") Unlike hairs, nails grow continuously throughout a person's life. On the average, nails grow about a tenth of a millimeter each day, but the rate of growth varies. Nail growth is fastest in the summer and slowest in the winter. The nails of babies and old people grow more slowly than those of young adults. Nail biting seems to make the nails grow faster. And the nails on different fingers grow at different rates: the thumbnails grow the fastest, and the nails on the little fingers the slowest. The size of the lunula at the base of the nail is an indication of how fast each nail grows. Little white spots on the nail (marks of minor bruises) move steadily down the fingertip as the nail grows.

Most mammals have narrow, pointed claws, but nearly all our monkey and ape relatives have flat nails. Nails are well suited to hands that are used for grasping and manipulating: they protect the fingertips from injury but don't have points to stick out and get in the way. Today most people keep their nails filed or clipped (or bitten) to a convenient length, and if the nails are allowed to grow very long normal everyday activities soon cause them to break. But some people in China, Japan and India used to let their nails grow very long. These were usually rich people or holy men—people who did not have to do any work with their hands. The longest nails ever recorded were grown by a man in India, whose left thumbnail alone was more than 27 inches long. (When nails are allowed to grow that long, they curve and loop into spirals like a ram's horns.) For the nobles of China, long nails were a symbol of their high station. Not only didn't they do any work with their hands; they couldn't! Their long nails were so awkward that they could not even eat without a servant's help. They wore nail guards of gold or silver to protect their long nails from breaking. Today some jewelry stores sell fake nails of real gold that can be attached with a special removable glue. But most people who want to decorate their nails use nail polish. Coloring the nails with red dyes has been in style in many parts of the world since ancient times.

The two outer layers of the skin, epidermis and dermis, rest on a supporting base of *subcutaneous tissue*. This tissue contains many cells that produce fat, and the fatty layer acts as a cushion and insulator. If you look at your hand, you will see a number of pronounced fat pads. There is one at the tip of each finger (including the thumb). Three fat pads cushion the end of the palm where the fingers are attached, and there is a large pad on the "heel" of the hand. There is a mound on the other side of the palm too, at the base of the thumb. But that is made of muscle, not fat. There is no fat under the skin in the center of the palm—the hollow of the hand. Few people realize how deep this hollow actually is. Hold your hand out straight, palm up, place a dime in the center of your palm, and then bet a friend that he or she can't brush off the coin with a clothes brush. This is a bet you are almost sure to win. The bristles of the brush will ride over the fat pads and muscular base of the thumb, leaving the dime safe in the hollow of your hand.

The hands are so active that they are the most likely parts of the body to have an accident. They are continually getting cut or burned or bruised. But their coat of skin is self-repairing. When it

32

is cut, for example, blood flows or oozes out but soon clots, forming a protective plug over the cut. Chemical signals are sent to the surrounding cells, and some of them move into the damaged area and multiply. Under the scab, new skin forms and grows to fill the gap. When the cut has healed, the scab falls off. If the cut is a small one, or if a burn is not very deep, the new skin that forms is a perfect copy of the skin that was damaged. But if the injury was more serious, the gap may be filled by connective tissue, which is made up mainly of the protein collagen. (Remember that this is the substance produced in the dermis, in the form of tough, strong fibers.) The wound has healed by the formation of a scar, which is pink at first but gradually fades to white. (Scar tissue does not contain any melanin-producing cells.) Scar tissue is not as elastic as normal skin. If the scars are large they may be pulled tight, hampering the movements of the hand.

Skin is constantly repairing and renewing itself. Usually the number of new cells formed is exactly enough to replace the old ones that are lost. But sometimes the system goes haywire, and cells continue to multiply even when no more are needed. Have you ever had a wart? It is a little patch of thickened skin. People have a lot of wrong ideas about warts. For example, they are not caused by touching a frog or toad; scientists have found that they are caused by a virus, which gets into a small nick or cut in the skin and then takes over, blocking the cells' normal turn-off signals so that they multiply. Many remedies have been tried, from reciting magic formulas to burning off the warts or freezing them with ultracold. The strange thing is that all of the methods, even the silliest—like burying potato peelings in a graveyard at midnight—do sometimes work. In fact, if a person with warts is hypnotized and told that the warts will disappear, they very likely will do so. Medical researchers have just recently begun to understand why this happens. A person's attitudes and emotions can have a strong effect on the immune system, the body's defense against invading germs—such as the virus that causes warts. If you really believe your warts will disappear, you may give your immune system enough of a boost to help it to get the virus under control.

Doctors find that the hands can give clues to diseases of the whole body. We have already mentioned the simian crease that may occur in Down's syndrome or a heart defect. Clubbed fingers, in which the fingertips are puffed and the moon end of the nail is raised, may be a sign of heart disease, respiratory diseases such as bronchitis or emphysema, an underactive thyroid gland, or cancer. A baby born with hammerhead nails may have cystic fibrosis. Sweaty hands and separation of the nail from the nail bed may be indications of thyroid problems. Unusually warm hands may mean the person has high blood pressure, gout, diabetes, hardening of the arteries, or rheumatoid arthritis. Cold hands can be an indication of anemia, problems with blood circulation, or shock. If your nails turn blue, you are not getting enough oxygen. Trembling hands can signal a variety of disorders, from too much to drink to senility, multiple sclerosis, or poisoning with heavy metals. White lines across the nail bed may indicate a liver disease such as cirrhosis. If half the nail turns white, the person may have kidney disease. But little white spots that gradually move down the nail as it grows are merely a sign of an injury to the nail bed.

34

3 / Hands: The Inside Story

A human hand can pat a cat, send a baseball hurtling toward the plate at more than ninety miles an hour, repair the tiny parts of a watch mechanism, and support the whole weight of a rock climber by the grip of the fingertips wedged into a small crack in the rock. How can one structure perform such feats of strength and dexterity? We have already found a part of the answer in the papillary ridges on the skin of the palms and fingertips, which help them to grip things firmly. But for the rest of the story we have to look inside the hand, at its inner skeleton of bones, at the muscles that move them, at the network of blood vessels that bring nourishment to the hand's living tissues, and at the nerves that link the hand with the brain.

Twenty-seven separate bones provide an inner framework for the human hand. First there are the eight wrist bones, or *carpals*. They look like little irregular-shaped pebbles, and they are arranged in two rows, fitted together like a mosaic. Each of the carpals has a name, as you can see in the picture. The names look rather complicated, but they are just Latin words describing the

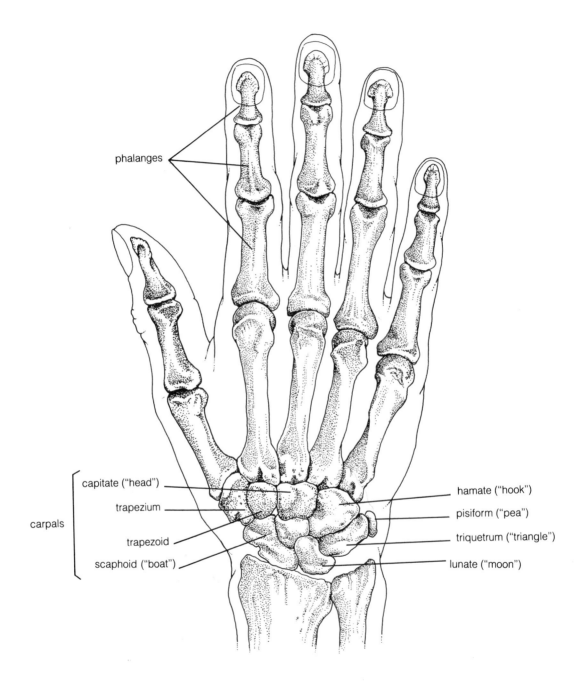

phalanges

carpals

capitate ("head")

trapezium

trapezoid

scaphoid ("boat")

hamate ("hook")

pisiform ("pea")

triquetrum ("triangle")

lunate ("moon")

shape of the bones—a boat, a moon, a triangle, a pea, two trapezoids, a little head and a hook. You can feel some of the individual carpal bones on the back of the wrist. Place a finger on the bony bump that sticks out on the little-finger side of the wrist and wag your hand back and forth. You will be able to feel two of the carpals sliding past each other as the hand turns.

When you look at an X-ray of the human hand, it looks a little strange. The fingers seem too long. The five long bones that branch out from the second row of carpals look like finger bones on an X-ray, but in a living hand they are joined by the flesh that forms the palm. These five long bones are called *metacarpals*.

Joined to the end of each metacarpal is a series of smaller and smaller bones. These are the real finger bones, the *phalanges*. (A single finger bone is called a *phalanx*.) The thumb has only two phalanges, but each of the fingers has three.

The bones of the hand are not firmly glued together. Instead, they are connected by joints that permit the bones to move. On the outside of the hand, you see the joints as knuckles. The ends of the bones are covered with soft, gristly *cartilage*, which keeps them from grinding together when the hands move. The whole joint is enclosed in a tough case called a *capsule*. Inside it the space around the bones is filled with a watery fluid that

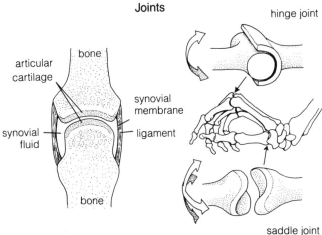

Joints

hinge joint

bone

articular
cartilage

synovial
membrane

synovial
fluid

ligament

bone

saddle joint

acts as a shock-absorbing cushion. The joints between the phalanges work like the hinges of a door. They permit only one kind of movement: back-and-forth. The joints that connect the metacarpals to the phalanges of the fingers permit two kinds of movement at right angles to each other. There is a hingelike back-and-forth movement when you close and open your hand, and there is a side-to-side movement when you spread your fingers and bring them together. (You can't bend any of the other finger joints side to side, no matter how hard you try.) The first phalanx of the thumb is connected to its metacarpal by a special kind of joint called a saddle joint. This kind of joint permits a great deal of movement: back and forth, from side to side, and around in a circle.

Bones cannot move by themselves; they are just supporting structures. They are moved by the action of *muscles.* Muscles are made up of cells that are naturally very "stretchy." When they relax they get longer, and when they contract they get shorter. The ends of the muscles are anchored to bones by tough, nonstretchy structures called *tendons.* Tendons may look like thin ropes or broad, flat sheets; either way, they are very strong. When muscles contract, they pull on the bones. Depending on how they are attached to the bones, they may make a joint open or close, or they may make bones move up, down, around, or from side to side.

Often muscles work in pairs—there is one to open a joint and another to close it, or one muscle to move bones apart and another to draw them together. The muscles of the hand are no exception. There is a whole set of *flexors,* which are muscles that bend the hand and fingers, and another set of *extensors,* muscles that straighten the

38

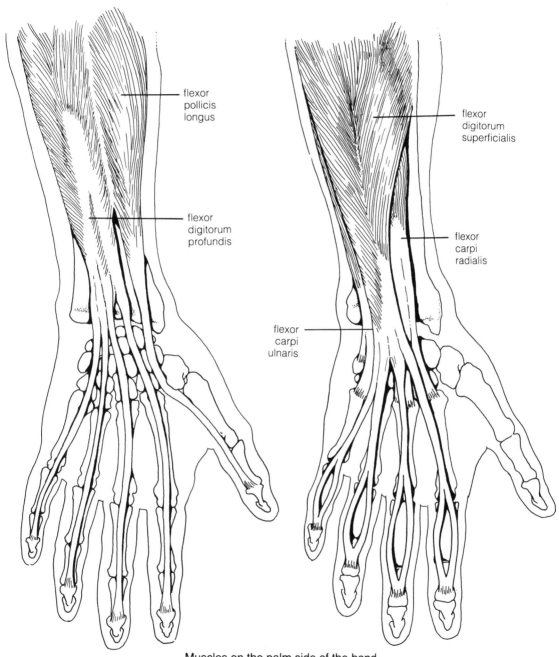

flexor
pollicis
longus

flexor
digitorum
profundis

flexor
digitorum
superficialis

flexor
carpi
radialis

flexor
carpi
ulnaris

Muscles on the palm side of the hand

hand and fingers. The flexors are found on the palm side of the hand. When they contract, they pull on the bones to which they are attached and make the hand close. They not only bend the joint, but also bring the fingers together. The extensors are on the back of the hand. When they contract and pull on the bones of the hand, they open the hand, pull the fingers out straight and spread them apart. If you straighten your hand and bend your fingers back as far as you can, you will see the long tendons of extensor muscles standing out on the back of your hand. In addition to the flexors and extensors, there are muscles that turn the hand palm up or palm down and other muscles that move the fingers and thumb.

There are thirty-eight muscles that move the hand. Nearly half of them are actually located outside the hand, in the forearm. At one end, short tendons attach these muscles to the bones of the elbow. At the other end, long tendons run down into the hand through a sort of tunnel in the carpal bones of the wrist and are attached to the metacarpals or phalanges. These forearm muscles act as flexors and extensors; they turn the hand palm up or palm down. The twenty muscles in the hand itself connect various parts of the hand. Some run from the carpals of the wrist to the metacarpals or phalanges. A group of muscles called *interossei* (meaning "between bones") spans the gaps between the metacarpals. Another group connects the tendons of flexor muscles to the tendons of extensors. There is even a special muscle connecting the muscles in the palm to the skin of the palm. All these muscles work together to produce the various movements of the hand.

Starting with your hand lightly closed, try pointing with your

40

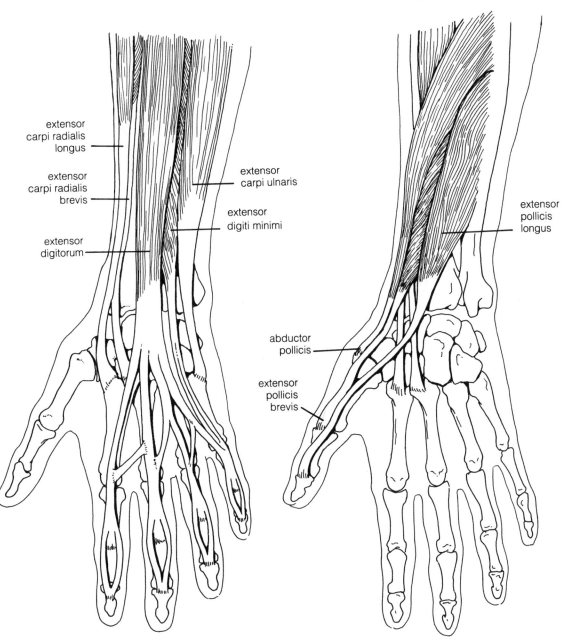

extensor
carpi radialis
longus

extensor
carpi radialis
brevis

extensor
digitorum

extensor
carpi ulnaris

extensor
digiti minimi

extensor
pollicis
longus

abductor
pollicis

extensor
pollicis
brevis

Muscles on the back of the hand

thumb without extending any of your fingers. That was easy, wasn't it? Now try pointing with your index finger, and then with your little finger, each time without extending any of the other fingers. Each of these movements was easy, too. But now try to point with your middle finger without moving any of your other fingers. That takes a great deal of effort. (You may actually have to hold your other fingers down with your thumb.) And you probably will not be able to extend your middle finger as much as you could your index finger. (Yet if you try to extend *both* index and middle fingers together, they go up easily.) If you try to point with your ring finger alone, you may not be able to straighten it at all.

Here's another puzzler. Extend both hands and hold them together in a "steeple," fingertips touching and thumb tips touching, but palms apart. Try moving your thumbs apart and back together again, and then do the same with each set of fingertips, one pair at a time. Now bend your middle fingers in so that the middle phalanges are resting against each other, while the tips of the other fingers and thumbs are still forming a steeple. Try to separate each pair of fingertips in turn, while still keeping the middle fingers clamped tightly together. You won't have any trouble moving your thumbs, index fingers or little fingers, but as soon as you try to move the tips of your ring fingers apart, the folded middle fingers will start to separate too. If you keep them together, you can't get your ring fingers apart!

What's the matter with your hands? Why don't the fingers all work the same way? The reason is that part of the muscles are shared by two or more fingers. When these muscles contract, *all* the fingers to which they are attached move together. In addition to the shared muscles, there are individual muscles that move certain fingers. The index finger has its own muscles, and so does the little finger. The thumb has a whole set of muscles to control its varied movements. But the middle finger and ring finger are moved mainly by shared muscles, and they tend to go where the other fingers go.

The bone structure of the human hand and the muscles that move the bones give the hand an ability that scientists call *prehensility*. A prehensile hand can grasp and manipulate things. With its opposable thumb and long, jointed fingers, the hand can grip things in several ways, each good for different uses.

The two main grips are the precision grip and the power grip. In the *precision grip* an object is held between the pads of the thumb and fingertips. If the object is large, all the fingers may be involved. Very small objects may be held by the thumb and index finger alone. The precision grip is good for tasks in which accuracy and delicacy are important, such as threading a needle, eating with a fork, pitching a baseball, or tying a bow. In the *power grip* an object is held between the surfaces of the fingers and the palms, with the thumb reinforcing the grip or guiding the action. The whole inner surfaces

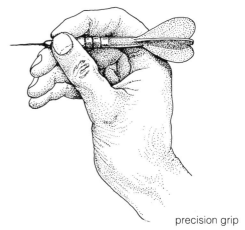

precision grip

power grip

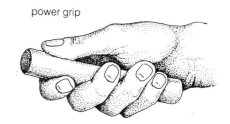

of the fingers (not just their tips) are in contact with the object, and the thumb may be wrapped over the backs of the fingers. You use a power grip when you hold a hammer or take a book off the shelf. In some actions you switch back and forth from one type of grip to the other. Replacing a light bulb, for example, you use the precision grip while you are trying to line up the threads in the socket, then gradually switch to a power grip when you screw in the bulb and tighten it.

A less often used grip that can be useful is the *hook grip*. An object is grasped with the fingers, which are bent tightly at the last two joints to form a hook. This grip is used in carrying a suitcase, pulling down a window from the top, or grasping pliers. When you pick up two billiard balls at the same time, you hold one in a precision grip between the thumb and the index and middle fingers, and the other in a curled hook formed by the other two fingers.

The *scissors grip* is another prehensile variation. An object is held between the side surfaces of the index and middle fingers. You don't get much power or accuracy with a scissors grip, but American smokers use it to hold a cigarette. (Smokers from other countries use variations of a thumb-and-finger pinch.) Contracting muscles, pulling on bones, make

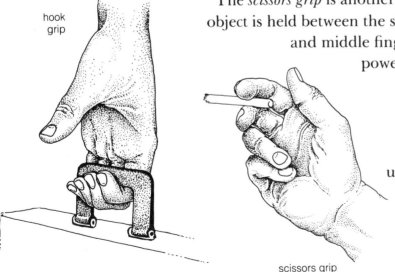

hook grip

scissors grip

the fingers and hands move. But what makes the muscles contract? Muscles contract in response to messages carried by nerves. Delicate threadlike nerves connect the muscles of the hands with the spinal cord and brain.

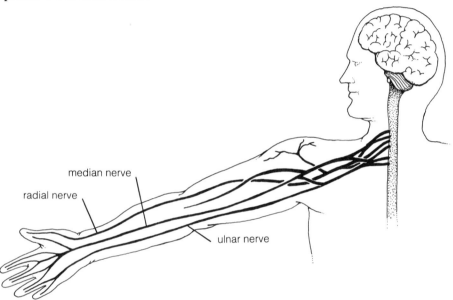

median nerve

radial nerve

ulnar nerve

Some nerves carry messages *to* the brain. These are *sensory nerves*, which carry information from the sense receptors. Touch, temperature and pain receptors gather information about the world outside the body—how warm or cold it is, whether there is an object in contact with the skin, and if so, whether it is soft or hard, wet or dry, rough or smooth. They give warnings if there is something dangerous—hot enough to burn or sharp enough to cut. The hand, like other parts of the body, also has some special sense receptors that gather information about what is going on inside the body. Receptors in the joints continually give the brain a

45

picture of exactly where the hands and fingers are, and whether they are moving. If you close your eyes and wave your hand about, move it behind your back, wiggle your fingers, pick up a pencil— you will know at all times just what your hand is doing, even though you can't see it.

Nerves called *motor nerves* carry messages *from* the brain and spinal cord. These are messages that tell muscles to contract and produce motion. Some actions are controlled by the spinal cord. When your pain receptors signal that you have put your hand on a hot stove, messages go flashing up sensory nerves to your spinal cord and from there to the brain. Before your brain has had a chance to receive and process the information—before you realize that your hand is getting burned—messages have flashed along motor nerves from the spinal cord, and you jerk your hand back, out of danger. A split second later, when your brain gets the message, you say "Ouch!"

Actions controlled by the spinal cord are called *reflex actions*. They are immediate, automatic responses to some urgent message, and they are usually rather simple actions. When you pull your hand away from a hot stove, you don't move it to anywhere in particular, just away, as quickly as possible. But the actions controlled by the brain can be very precise and finely coordinated. Two parts of the brain are concerned with controlling the actions of muscles: the *cerebrum* (the thinking brain), which directs the actions; and the *cerebellum*, a structure at the back of the brain, which coordinates movements. If you decide to pick up a glass of milk and drink from it, the cerebrum sends out signals that make muscles contract to reach out with your hand, close your fingers around the glass, and lift it to your mouth. Signals carried along nerves from the cerebellum tell the muscles how much to contract and when to stop, so that you don't knock over the glass or tip the milk down the front of your shirt instead of into your mouth.

The brain cells in the cerebrum that send messages to the muscles are located in two strips that run down the outer surface of each side of the brain. These control centers are called the *motor strips*. Scientists have found that messages from a certain part of the motor strip control the muscles of the hands, those from another

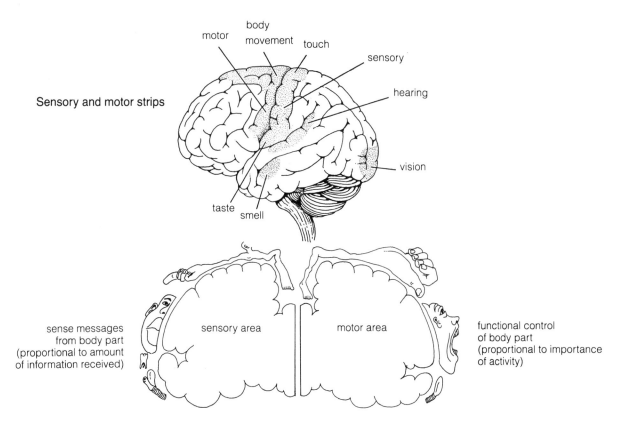

Sensory and motor strips

part control the muscles of the face, and so on. They have made maps of which parts of the motor strips control which parts of the body. You might expect that a large part of the body would correspond to a large part of the motor strip, and a small part to a small one. But that is not so. Instead, the amount of space on the motor strip corresponds to the number of muscles in the body part and how varied and complicated their actions are. So the control area for the hand is much larger than you might expect from its size—almost as large as the control area for the whole chest and belly. Next to the motor strip on each side of the brain there is a *sensory strip*, where sense messages from various parts of the body are received and processed. Here too, messages from the hand take up much more brain space than the size of the hand would suggest.

There is something odd about the way the nerves that carry messages to and from the brain are connected. Most of these nerves cross over to the opposite side at the bottom of the brain. So the left side of the brain receives messages about what is happening on the right side of the body, and the right side of the brain receives messages from the left side of the body. The movements of your right hand are controlled by the left side of your brain, while those of your left hand are controlled by your right brain. Nerves that connect the two halves of the brain let the whole brain know what is going on in both halves of the body.

If something happens to interrupt the flow of messages from the brain to the hands, they will become *paralyzed*, unable to move. A cutoff of sensory messages to the brain will make the hands feel numb, without their normal senses of touch, temperature and

48

pain. A broken neck may result in paralysis of all parts of the body whose nerves reach the spinal cord below the damage. This may include the hands. Sometimes a pinched nerve may cause a more limited paralysis. In a condition called *carpal tunnel syndrome*, the tissues of the wrist become inflamed and press on the nerves that run through the carpal tunnel along with the muscle tendons. Tingling, pain and numbness of the thumb and fingers may result. Often these symptoms occur at night, after the person has gone to bed. Concert pianist Leon Fleisher had a worldwide reputation when he began to suffer from numbness in the fingers of his right hand. Soon he found he was hitting wrong notes and couldn't stretch his fingers to play the chords he used to handle with ease. After years of playing only concertos for the left hand and consulting a series of doctors, Fleisher finally found out that he was suffering from carpal tunnel syndrome. Surgery to repair the damaged tissues and special exercises to strengthen the hand muscles restored much of his lost skill, and he gave a triumphant two-handed concert in 1982.

Skin, muscles, bone and nerves—these are all living tissues that need continual supplies of energy and food materials to power their activities and repair damage. The food materials and oxygen that living cells need are carried by the blood, which flows through tubelike blood vessels. *Arteries* are blood vessels that carry blood away from the heart to the body. They branch and rebranch into smaller and smaller tubes, finally forming *capillaries*, which are tubes so tiny you need a microscope to see them. The capillaries have very thin walls. Oxygen and food substances pass out of them

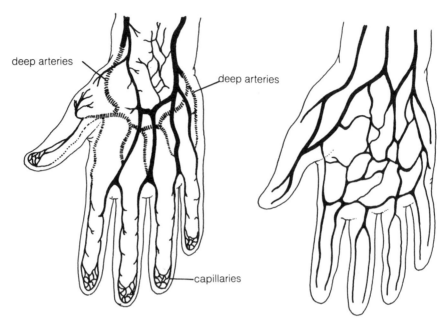

arteries   veins

deep arteries

deep arteries

capillaries

Major blood vessels of the hand

into the cells, and carbon dioxide and other waste products pass out of the cells into the capillaries. The capillaries join to form larger and larger tubes, eventually producing *veins*, blood vessels that carry blood back to the heart. The oxygen-rich blood that the arteries carry to the body is bright red.

You can't see any arteries when you look at your hand because they are buried deep inside the tissues. (One artery, the radial artery, passes close to the surface at the wrist. When you take your pulse there, you are feeling the strong, steady contractions of the muscular walls of the artery as they help to pump the blood along.)

If you shine a flashlight through the tip of your finger, your flesh will glow a bright ruby red. The color comes from the blood flowing through tiny capillaries. You can see the paths of some of the veins that carry blood back from your hand. They appear as blue lines on the palm and the back of the hand. Veins appear blue because the blood they carry is darker than the bright-red arterial blood. Veins do not have thick, muscular walls, and blood flows in them rather sluggishly. If you let your hand hang down, you will see the veins in the back of your hand bulge out. Blood is pooling in them and filling them. Now raise your hand above your shoulder. As you watch, the bulging veins seem to disappear. The back of your hand is smooth, and only faint blue lines show the paths of the veins. With your hand up, gravity has helped to empty the veins, sending the blood back down your arm toward the heart.

In the preceding chapter we mentioned that the body can get rid of excess heat by sweating. The blood that flows in capillaries close to the surface of the skin also radiates heat out into the air. Normally the hands feel comfortably warm as a result of the heat carried by their rich blood supply. But when you go into a cold place, the body switches on its heat-conserving system. Some of the blood vessels feeding the capillaries in the hands and feet close down and send the blood back toward the heart. That way the amount of heat lost by radiation through the skin is decreased. Even though the hands and feet are cold, the rest of the body—including important organs like the brain—is kept warm. In people suffering from a condition called *Raynaud's syndrome,* the body's temperature-control switches overwork. When the temperature outside the body is cold, so much of the circulation to the hands and feet is cut off that they become very cold and pale. Tissues may even be damaged, for lack of nourishing blood.

Cold is not the only thing that can cut down the circulation of blood to the hands. When you are digesting a large meal, extra blood is shunted to the stomach and intestines to help in their work, and your hands may feel a bit cold. During a migraine headache, blood vessels in the head are swollen and throbbing, and the person's hands are usually very cold. Some migraine sufferers can learn by biofeedback training to consciously increase the blood flow to the hands. This drains blood away from the painfully swollen blood vessels in the head and stops the ache.

We tend to take the amazing dexterity of our hands for granted. But for the millions of people whose hands are crippled by *arthritis,* everyday tasks—buttoning a button or cutting food with a knife and fork, for example—may become difficult or impossible. Arthritis is a disease of the joints. There are several types. The most common are rheumatoid arthritis and osteoarthritis.

Rheumatoid arthritis is an inflammation of the joints. The joint membranes become swollen and produce extra fluid, which causes the joints to become swollen, stiff and painful. Scientists now believe that rheumatoid arthritis is caused by a virus, but it also seems to be influenced by heredity. It can strike people of any age, from children up to the very old. The pain and stiffness tend to be worst in the morning, and then the joints loosen up as the day goes on. There may also be fever and a generally miserable feeling. Sufferers report that they feel more pain and stiffness when the

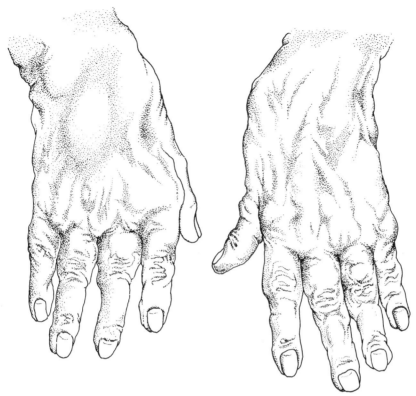

hands suffering from arthritis

humidity rises and the barometric pressure falls. Their aching joints seem to act like weather forecasters, predicting rain.

Osteoarthritis is a form of damage to the joints that develops as a result of wear and tear. The cartilage that protects the ends of the bones thins, cracks and breaks away. Then the bone ends roughen and thicken, and the joints become swollen and painful. Osteoarthritis is mainly a disease of older people, but it can develop in anyone whose joints are subjected to unusual stress, such as athletes and ballet dancers. Someone who uses the hands a great deal, as in sewing or typing, may develop osteoarthritis in the joints of the hand and fingers.

A combination of treatments works best on arthritis. Aspirin or other drugs are used to reduce the pain, swelling and inflammation. Meanwhile, the person follows a program of rest and careful exercise to restore movement to the joint. Swimming and other exercises in water are especially helpful.

4 / Left Hand, Right Hand

People are very concerned these days about discrimination and the rights of minority groups. But there is one misunderstood and mistreated minority that has not made much progress toward winning equal rights. That is the left-handers. In the United States they make up about 10 percent of the population.

It is hard to be a left-hander in a right-handed world. Everyday objects, from the desks in school to can openers and golf clubs, are designed for convenient use by right-handers. When a right-hander holds a pair of scissors, the natural pressures of the fingers hold the blades closed, and they cut cleanly. But a left-hander's fingers tend to force the blades of scissors apart, and they hack unevenly at a paper instead of cutting it. Guitars are strung for fingering with the left hand while the right hand takes the more active role of strumming. Wrist watches that need winding have the stem on the right side, and digital watches have their controls on the right. They are meant to be worn on the left arm, leaving the right arm free for more important tasks.

Even our language is full of slurs against left-handers. The word

sinister, meaning "evil" and "menacing," comes from the Latin for "left." The French word for "left," *gauche,* is used to mean "clumsy" and "awkward." A "left-handed compliment" is an insult. Meanwhile, *right* is a synonym for "correct." We say someone who is clever and skillful is *adroit* (from the French for "right") or possesses great *dexterity* (from the Latin for "right"). Someone who can use both hands with equal ease is said to be *ambidextrous,* implying that he or she has two right hands!

Still, left-handers do have some advantages. Left-handed boxers and tennis players may confuse their opponents, who are used to competing against right-handers. Typewriter keyboards are designed with more of the commonly used letters on the left. And left-handers are often very intelligent and talented people. Left-handed achievers have included Alexander the Great; artists Michelangelo and Leonardo da Vinci; writers Lewis Carroll (the author of *Alice in Wonderland*) and Samuel Clemens (better known as Mark Twain); movie stars Charlie Chaplin, Judy Garland, Kim

Novak and Robert Redford; sports stars Babe Ruth, Mark Spitz and Jimmy Connors; and astronaut Wally Schirra.

Are you left-handed or right-handed? You probably answered that question on the basis of the hand you use for writing. But that may not necessarily be the hand you use for other tasks. With which hand do you throw a ball? Which hand do you use to button or zip up your clothes? Which hand do you use for eating? Many people use one hand for certain tasks and the other hand for others. (We have a daughter who writes and eats with her right hand but throws balls with her left.) Even if you use the same hand for all important tasks, you may be doing so because you were taught that way. In some countries children are not permitted to write with the left hand; they are forced to learn to write with the right hand, whether they want to or not. In Arab countries the left hand is considered "unclean"; it is used for toilet functions, and only the right hand can be used for eating and other respectable tasks. (The reasons behind that custom seem more understandable if you consider that in those countries water for washing may be scarce, and people eat with their hands from a common food bowl.) Even in the United States, where we are more inclined to let people "do their own thing," parents may place a spoon in a young child's right hand because they are used to doing things that way. Or they may teach a child the right-handed way to sew or play a musical instrument because it is too hard to figure out how to do it the opposite way.

There are some simple tests that indicate which hand you tend to favor and how consistent you are in your handedness:

Handedness tests

1. Draw a circle with your right hand. Did you move the pencil clockwise or counterclockwise? Now draw a circle with your left hand. Which way did you move the pencil this time? (With each hand, try to draw the circle the way that "feels right," without thinking too much about it beforehand.)

2. Draw the head of an animal, such as a dog or a horse, facing toward the side. Is your drawing facing to the left or the right?

3. Clap your hands as though you are applauding for a performer. Which hand is on top, clapping into the other?

4. Grasp your hands behind your head. Which hand grasped the other?

5. Which foot do you use to kick a ball?

6. Hold one arm out straight, with your index finger pointing upward. Look at your index finger and close one eye. Did the finger seem to move to the side? Now try the same test with the other eye. Which eye was open when your finger seemed to stay in the same place as it was when you were looking with both eyes?

This is what your answers mean:

1. Most right-handers draw circles counterclockwise, no matter which hand is holding the pencil. Most left-handers draw circles clockwise.
2. Right-handers tend to draw faces pointing to the left, and left-handers draw them facing right.
3. The hand that is on top when you clap is your dominant hand.
4. If your right hand grasped your left, you favor your right hand. If your left hand grasped your right, your left hand is dominant.
5. The foot that you kick with is your dominant foot. Usually the dominant hand and foot are on the same side, but this is not always the case.
6. The eye that saw your finger in the same position as when you were using two eyes is your dominant eye. Usually (but not always) the dominant hand and eye are on the same side.

If you answered "right" for all the questions, then you are a very strong right-hander. If you answered "left" for all the questions, you are a very strong left-hander. If your answers were mixed, then the side with the most answers is the one you tend to favor. If your answers were split about half and half, or if you answered "left" to many of the questions but write with your right hand, then you may be a natural left-hander who was changed by parents or teachers.

Why do people tend to favor one hand over the other? And why are most people right-handed rather than left-handed? Scientists have looked at various kinds of evidence, and they have come up with some possible explanations.

First of all, studies of other animals often give clues to how things work in humans. Some chickens peck more to one side than to the other, but there is not much difference between the number who prefer the left and those who tend to peck toward the right. Cats use a paw to pat and cuff a mouse they have cornered, or to play with a ball of yarn dangled by their owner. Some cats seem to be right-pawed, about the same number are left-pawed, and some use either paw. In experiments in which laboratory mice had to reach into a tube with a paw to get a food reward, most of the mice showed a preference for one paw over the other. About half were right-pawed, and half were lefties. Somewhat different results were found in studies of our closer relatives, monkeys and apes. Both wild chimpanzees and chimps raised by humans show a definite handedness, with more left-handers than right-handers. Monkeys also seem to prefer the left hand.

What about our human relatives? Many stone tools made by prehistoric people have been found. More of these tools were made to be held in the right hand than were made for the left, although the difference is much smaller than today's nine-to-one ratio in favor of right-handers. Pictures of hands made on cave walls also suggest that right-handers were in the majority in the Stone Age.

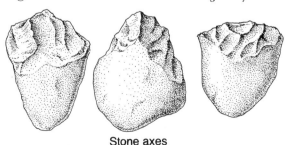

Stone axes

Cave paintings

When the pictures were made by dipping a hand in paint and pressing it against the wall to make a handprint, the hand was usually a right hand. But pictures made by tracing the outline of a hand with a finger dipped in paint usually show a left hand. (The left hand served as the model while the right hand drew the outline). Beautiful paintings of animals and hunters made in caves by prehistoric artists usually show the animals facing toward the right, though. This would seem to indicate that left-handers drew them. But even if this is true, all it proves is that left-handers were in the majority among the *artists,* not necessarily among the cave people in general.

There were some advantages to having most of the members of the community favor the same hand. Tools were handed down from one generation to another, or shared by the community. A left-hander would be at a disadvantage trying to use tools made for right-handers, so those who went along with the majority had a better chance to survive. Some other theories have been suggested to explain why right-handers were favored rather than left-handers. Ancient people had the mistaken idea that the heart is on the left side of the body. (Actually it is in the middle of the chest, but tipped so that the heartbeat is felt on the left.) So, fighters held their shields on the left to protect the heart and used the right hand to hold their swords. Women had a different reason for being right-handed. Most women hold their babies cradled in the crook of the left arm, leaving the right hand free. Even left-handed women do this, because a baby held on its mother's left can hear her familiar heartbeat and is quieter and more contented.

Is handedness hereditary? Or is it learned? Studies suggest that heredity does play a role. So does early training, which may change some lefties to righties. But there seems to be something else involved, too. Babies who suffered minor brain damage at birth are about twice as likely to be left-handed as the rest of the population. Doctors now think that there are some "natural" left-handers, but others are natural right-handers who became left-handed because of an injury to the brain while it was developing.

The brain seems to be the key to handedness. Studies of people who have had a stroke or an injury that damaged part of the brain and experiments in which parts of the brain were stimulated with electricity during an operation have made it possible to map which parts of the brain control the various kinds of activity. These studies have shown that the human brain is *lateralized*—that is, the two sides of the brain tend to specialize in different things. In most people the centers for speech and for understanding language are found in the left half of the brain. This is the dominant half of the brain, and it is strong in orderly, analytical thinking. The left brain is good at complicated arithmetic and problem solving. The right brain does not have much verbal ability, although it can understand simple words and do simple arithmetic. But it is good at recognizing shapes and their relationships to one another, and it has a strong artistic sense. The right brain is also concerned with musical rhythm and melody. It too can solve problems, but not the way the left brain does. Instead of taking problems step by step, the right brain sees the whole picture and takes leaps of insight and intuition.

Do you recall that the brain receives and sends messages in a crisscross fashion? The right hand is controlled by the left brain, and the left hand is controlled by the right brain. Scientists suggested that the right-handed majority have their speech center in the left brain, which is the dominant half. Left-handers, on the contrary, would have a dominant right brain, with the speech center located there. In most cases this is true. But some left-handers have a dominant left brain, just as most right-handers do. A small number of right-handers have their speech center on the right side. And some people's brains are not completely lateralized; they have centers for speech on both sides of the brain. This is especially true of left-handers. (The confusion between these competing centers would explain why left-handers are more likely to suffer from stuttering than right-handers.)

Scientists use complicated and expensive equipment to determine which side of the brain is dominant. But Jerre Levy, a psychologist at the University of Pennsylvania, found that a simple test can reveal the dominant side of the brain. All you need for the test is a pencil and a piece of paper.

Write a few words on the paper, using your normal writing hand,

and watch your hand as it moves. Is the pencil point pointing toward you or away from you? Is your hand below the line of writing, or is it curled up above it? People use two main writing techniques: straight and hooked. If you are a straight writer, you hold your hand below the line and your pencil points away from you. If you are a hooked writer, you curl your hand up over the line and hold the pencil pointing toward you. Many left-handers use the hooked writing style, and it was suggested that they do this to get the writing hand out of the way, so it won't smear the writing. But there are left-handers who use the straight style, and there are hooked-writing right-handers. And most right-handers who write

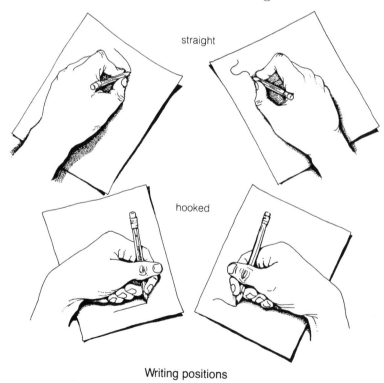

straight

hooked

Writing positions

in Hebrew, which goes from right to left, hold their hands straight even though they would have the same smearing problems as a left-hander writing from left to right. Jerre Levy found that the way you hold your hand when you write depends on which side of your brain is dominant:

Straight right-handers have a dominant left brain.
Hooked left-handers also have a dominant left brain.
Straight left-handers have a dominant right brain.
Hooked right-handers also have a dominant right brain.

So, only the people (both right-handers and left-handers) who use the straight writing style have the normal crisscross relationship between the dominant brain and dominant hand. The hooked-handers tend to have some of their speech and other abilities divided between the two halves of the brain.

An organization called Lefthanders International is working to win more respect for lefties. It publishes a magazine, *Lefty*, with articles on research into handedness and the achievements of successful left-handers. The organization also keeps an updated listing of stores and catalogs that specialize in products designed for left-handers, from left-handed scissors to instructions for left-handed handcrafts and sports to mugs and bumper stickers with slogans like "LEFTYS DO IT BETTER."

5 / Let Your Fingers Do The Talking

Our local newspaper recently ran a story about the first deaf juror ever to serve in New Jersey. All through the trial an interpreter translated the testimony into sign language for the deaf woman and then helped her to communicate with the other jurors while they were deciding on their verdict.

For millions of deaf people, hands provide the only means of communicating with others. But even for people with normal hearing, gestures of the hands can add meaning to speech or substitute for spoken words. Watch people when they are talking— in the lunchroom, on a street corner, on a bus. As they talk, their hands move in gestures that are often easy to follow: a pointed finger, a hand chopping down for emphasis, an angry fist, hands spread wide to indicate puzzlement. Some people gesture more than others, depending on their personality and especially on their racial or national background. In the American "melting pot," people of Jewish and Italian backgrounds are especially noted for talking with their hands. Their varied and vivid gestures may seem overdone to the more restrained people of English descent. In general, people from hot climates tend to gesture more than those from cold climates. And as people climb the social ladder, their use of gestures grows more limited, no matter what their ethnic background.

Some gestures seem almost universal, like the finger placed over the lips in a "Sh-h" sign. But many gestures mean different things in different cultures, and their use by travelers can cause misunderstandings. Take the wave, for example. Variations of waving are used as greetings when you meet someone and as a parting salute when you leave. You may wave with your hand flapping up and down, or raise it in an Indian "How!" salute, or wag it back and forth like a window wiper. These are typical American gestures, but on the European continent people are more likely to greet each other with the right hand raised and the fingers and thumb flapping together and apart like a set of chattering teeth. In France

this "Continental wave" is made with the palm facing the person being greeted. Italians and Greeks make the gesture with the palm facing away from the person being greeted; in their countries an open palm is a symbol for the evil eye, and a wave with the palm showing is an insult.

Thumbing your nose at someone—putting the tip of your thumb to your nose and fanning out your fingers—is universally understood as a mocking insult. But people disagree on whether it means "You're a big baby" (the gesture looks something like sucking a thumb), "You have an ugly long nose," or "You smell bad." Some people see the gesture as a mock salute ("Oops! My hand slipped.") or think it is an imitation of the fanning of a cock's comb.

If you want to say, "He's crazy!" you may tap your forehead or make circles with your forefinger at your temple. But in some countries tapping the temple means "He's smart," and in Mediterranean countries the gesture for craziness is made by putting the thumb to the temple and twisting the hand back and forth.

The ring sign is a gesture found all over the world. You make it by bringing the tips of your thumb and index finger together to form a circle. To most people that gesture means something like "O.K.," "good," "perfect," or "ready to go." But for some it is a

symbol for a hole, especially one of the openings in the body, and it is used as a rude insult. In France the ring gesture is a symbol for zero, and it is used to indicate that something is worthless.

The "thumbs up" sign means O.K. to most people. But some use it to mean the number one. Americans use the thumbs-up gesture when they hitchhike ("thumbing a ride"), but they can get into trouble if they use it in Greece or Sardinia, where the thumbing gesture is an insult. There hitchhikers ask a car to stop with a flat hand wave. Most people think the O.K. meaning of the thumbs-up gesture came from ancient Rome, where the audience signaled whether a fallen gladiator was to be killed or spared. Thumbs up meant he should live, and thumbs down meant he deserved to die. Actually, though, the fans at the Roman games signaled "kill" with their thumbs out (mimicking a sword) and "spare him" with the thumb tucked into the fist. Mistranslations of the old descriptions of the games led to the change in the gesture.

Crossed fingers are another example of a gesture whose meaning has changed. This was originally a symbol of the Christian cross. In Mediterranean countries, the forefingers of the two hands are held across each other in a superstitious gesture against vampires or the evil eye. In South America the cross is made with the thumb and forefinger. But in the United States and Northern European countries the middle finger is crossed over the index finger. We cross our fingers to bring us good luck, or to swear our good faith, but sometimes we cross our fingers when we tell a lie.

One person can start the use of a symbol. During World War II, the British Prime Minister Winston Churchill invented the "V for

Victory" sign, in which the index and middle fingers are held up, spread to form a V, and the other fingers are folded over. The correct way to make this sign is with the palm turned toward the viewer. The same V with the back of the hand facing the viewer is a crude insult.

The handshake is an important gesture in our culture. It can be used in greeting, in farewell, as a congratulation, and as a mark of agreement. ("Let's shake on it!") In the usual form of the handshake, two people face each other, clasp right hands (with the thumb separated from the fingers), and move them up and down. The length of the handshake and the number of up-and-down strokes may be an indication of a person's ethnic background and social status. People from the Midwest tend to pump heartily up and down five or six times; Easterners, especially those of Anglo-Saxon ancestry, are more likely to cut the greeting short after one or two shakes (or even just a single downstroke).

Queens, starlets, politicians' wives, and various other people who must shake hands hundreds of times in an hour typically use a soft, quiet clamp. Politicians, on the other hand, use their handshakes to win votes, and their typical style is a hearty clasp, often with the left hand covering the clasp or giving an encouraging squeeze to the other person's arm or shoulder. Athletes may use a one- or two-handed slap or a double-handed clasp for greeting or congratulation. Generally people get a positive feeling from a handshake that is cool, dry and firm. The "dead fish," a handshake that is cold, clammy and limp, gives the impression that the person shaking your hand doesn't care about you. The "bonecrusher," a squeeze so powerful that it is painful, is usually the mark of someone trying to prove his manliness. Clubs and societies may have variations on the basic handshake that provide a kind of recognition test for people of similar interests or beliefs.

Shaking hands is an old custom that dates back to the days when most men carried weapons. A handshake was a sign of peace, an indication that two people were willing to talk without weapons in their hands. Native Americans hold up their right hand as a peace greeting; Orientals hold out both hands, palms upward.

Our hands can reveal things that we intended to keep hidden. Nervous habits like drumming on a tabletop or playing with a lock of hair may indicate uneasiness or boredom. When a man is perplexed he may rub his chin, nose, forehead or neck, or tug at his earlobes. A woman has different mannerisms to indicate the same feelings; she may place a finger under her chin or put the tip of her index finger on her lower teeth with the mouth slightly open. A person who is telling a lie is likely to touch the face frequently while talking, especially covering the mouth or touching the nose. And people who pick their teeth or noses in public are sending the message that they haven't learned the accepted manners—or don't care what people think of them.

When people cannot communicate with speech, hand gestures can provide an excellent substitute. Native Americans had a well-developed sign language, used when different tribes with different spoken languages gathered for a meeting. Today, tourists in foreign countries often invent their own gestures by pantomime to make themselves understood. Placing the hands together horizontally and laying the head on them, for example, would mean "I need a place to sleep."

If you have seen the movie *The Miracle Worker*, you probably have a vivid memory of the exciting moment when the young Helen Keller, deaf and blind, finally understood the word "water" spelled out on her palm. Several different systems are now being used to teach deaf children, and a great debate is going on about which one is the best.

Some people believe that deaf children should be taught to read lips and to speak, and then they should go to school with children who have normal hearing. The problem with that theory is that many deaf children have trouble learning lipreading. They learn slowly and tend to be behind in their schoolwork, even if they are very bright. After years of practice, lipreading is still a guessing game, and some key words may be missed. Picture this scene, for example: A husband comes home from work and asks, "Where is the baby?" His deaf wife, reading his lips, thinks he said, "Where is the paper?" (B's and p's look alike when they are formed by the lips.) "I threw it in the wastebasket," the wife answers.

Recently a new technique called *cued speech* has been invented to take the guesswork out of lipreading. The speaker uses hand signals to distinguish between look-alike sounds like b, p, and m. Deaf children taught with cued speech quickly learn to use language and soon are reading and writing too.

Many deaf people believe there is an even better way to open up deaf children's minds to language. Instead of relying on spoken words, they start from the very beginning, teaching the children to speak with their hands.

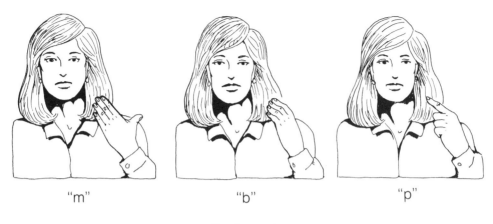

"m"　　　　　"b"　　　　　"p"

Cued speech

In *finger spelling* there is a hand position for each letter of the alphabet. Words are spelled out, using these hand gestures.

But spelling every word is a slow way to communicate. Another hand language, like the sign language of the American Indians, uses gestures for whole words. This language is called *American Sign Language*, often abbreviated as *Ameslan* or *ASL*. The idea of having to learn a different gesture for every word may sound impossibly difficult at first. But many of the signs in Ameslan are "natural" signs, easily understood and easy to learn. For exam~~
you say "I love you" in sign language by holding yo~~
arms wrapped tightly in front of you. A~~
with its own vocabulary and gram~~
used language in the United S~~
Italian. Children learn it quick~~
large as those of normal-b~~
speech. Children raised in A~~
naturally, usually before th~~

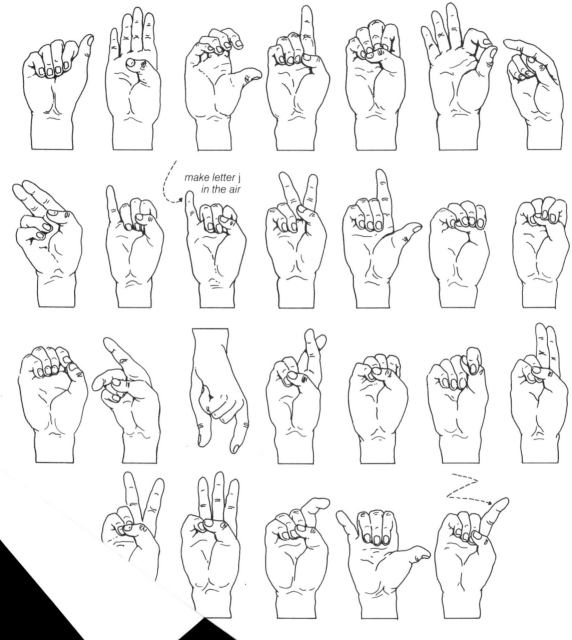

make letter j
in the air

finger spelling

hear   look   Are you ill?   key   fruit

Ameslan signs

Many deaf people believe that signing is the best way to teach deaf children. But there is a problem. People who know only Ameslan and cannot lip-read are unable to communicate with most people with normal hearing. They tend to stay in a tight little community of the deaf, where they can be understood and feel comfortable. Signing is so easy that deaf children who have learned Ameslan may not cooperate with teachers who try to teach them to lip-read. Later, when they must go out into the hearing world and work for a living, they are at a great disadvantage.

The debate will probably continue for some time. Meanwhile, American Sign Language has had an unexpected application. Scientists had wondered for a long time just how intelligent our ape relatives really are, and whether they have the ability to use language. Attempts to teach chimpanzees to speak have had very limited success. With great effort, a chimpanzee can be taught to say a few simple words, but its mouth and throat simply aren't built for complicated speech.

Language studies with chimpanzees seemed to have reached a dead end until researchers got the idea of teaching them sign language. The apes' nimble hands mastered the signs of Ameslan with ease. One of the earliest chimpanzees to learn sign language, a young female named Washoe, built up a sign vocabulary of more

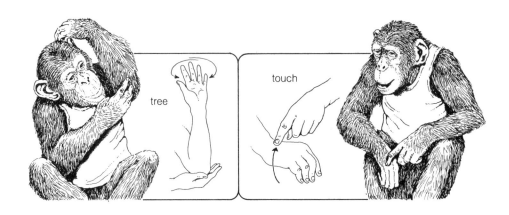

than a hundred words and put them together into two-word sentences like "Please tickle" and "Washoe sorry." Sometimes she invented signs of her own. One day she asked for her bib by drawing the outline of a bib on her chest. Her human teachers couldn't find a symbol for bib in their Ameslan dictionaries, so they made one up and tried to teach it to Washoe. Later they discovered that the sign the chimpanzee had used was really the correct sign for bib.

After Washoe grew up, the researchers gave her a young orphan chimpanzee, Louis, to raise. Soon Louis too was learning Ameslan, picking up signs by imitating his foster mother just as a human child learns to speak by imitating its parents. Studies of Washoe and other Ameslan-speaking apes are bringing us new knowledge about language and about the minds of our closest animal relatives.

Thus, the story of your hand has proved to be far more varied and wide-ranging than you might have suspected. A multipurpose tool, a sense organ, and even an organ of communication, the hand takes part in almost every aspect of human activity.

Index

Note: Numbers in *italics* refer to illustrations.

Alexander the Great, 56
American Indian sign language, 71
American Sign Language (ASL),
   73, 75. *See also* Ameslan
Ameslan, 73, 75, *75*, 76
arch, 20, *20*
arteries, 49, 50, *50*
arthritis, 52, 53, *53*, 54

biofeedback, 52
blood circulation in hands, 49–52
blue hands, 34
Boleyn, Ann, 15
bones of hands, 35, *36*, 37, *37*, 38
brain, 45, 47, *47*, 48
brain dominance, 62–65

Caesar, Julius, 17–18
callus, 9, 14
capillaries, 49, 50, *50*, 51
capitate, *36*
carpal tunnel, 40
carpal tunnel syndrome, 49
carpals, 35, *36*, 37
Carroll, Lewis, 56
cartilage, 37
cats, 60
cave paintings, 60–61, *61*
cerebellum, 46, 47
cerebrum, 46, 47, *47*

Chaplin, Charlie, 56
chickens, 60
chimpanzees, 9, *10*, 11, 60, 75–76
   learn sign language, 75, 76
Churchill, Winston, 69
clubbed fingers, 34
cold hands, 34, 51
collagen, *22*, 23, 33
communication, 13, 66–76
Connors, Jimmy, 57
continental wave, 67, *67*, 68
corneal layer of skin, 21, *22*
crossed fingers, *68*, 69
cued speech, *72*, 73

deaf, 66, 71–75
de Larrocha, Alicia, 15
dermis, *22*, 23–24
digit, 15–17
Down's syndrome, 19

ectrodactyly, 15, *15*
epidermis, 21–22, *22*
extensors, 38, 40, *41*

FBI, 20, 24
Fleisher, Leon, 49
fingernail, 30, *30*, 31, 32
fingerprints, 19, 20, *20*
fingers, 15, *15*, 16–17

finger spelling, 73, 74
flexors, 38, *39*
flexure lines, 17–19
follicle, 29, *29*
foot-hands, 9, *10,* 11
freckles, 23

Garland, Judy, 56
gestures, 12, 66–72
Goodall, Jane, 9
gorilla, 9, 11
gripping, 21, 25, 43, *43,* 44, *44*

hair, 24, 25, 29, *29,* 30
hamate, *36*
hammerhead nail, 34
handedness, 55–65
  tests for, 58–59
handshake, 70–71
head line, 18, *18*
healing, 33
heart line, 18, *18*
heat radiation, 51
heel of hand, 32
heredity of handedness, 62
hinge joint, *37,* 38
hook grip, 44, *44*
hooked writing, 64, *64,* 65
Hoover, J. Edgar, 24
How! sign, 67

index finger, *15,* 16, 42, 43
interossei, 40

joints, 37, *37,* 38

Keller, Helen, 72
keratin, 21, 22, 29, 30
knuckle walking, 9, *10,* 11

knuckles, 17, 37

lateralization of brain, 62–65
left-handers, 55–57, 65
Lefthanders International, 65
Lefty magazine, 65
Leonardo da Vinci, 56
Levy, Jerre, 63, 65
lifeline, 18, *18*
lipreading, 72, 73, 75
little finger, *15,* 16, 42, 43
loop, 20, *20*
Louis, 76
lunate, *36*
lunula, *30,* 31

map of skin senses, 25–27, *26*
median nerve, *45*
melanin, 23
metacarpals, *36,* 37
mice, 60
Michelangelo, 56
middle finger, *15,* 16, 42, 43
migraine, 52
Miracle Worker, The, 72
monkeys, 9, *10,* 60. *See also*
  chimpanzees; gorillas
motor nerves, 46
motor strips, 47, *47,* 48
muscles of hand, 38, *39,* 40, *41,*
  42, 43

nail bed, 30, *30*
nerves, 45, *45,* 46
Novak, Kim, 56–57

opposable thumb, 8
orangutans, 9
osteoarthritis, 53–54

palm, 17, 18, *18,* 19, 68
  mapping senses of, 25–26,
  26
palmistry, 17–18, *18*
papillae, *22,* 23
papillary ridges, 19, 20, 21
paralysis, 48, 49
phalanges, *36,* 37
pinkie, 16
pisiform, *36*
polydactyly, 15, *15*
power grip, 43, *43,* 44
precision grip, 43, *43*
prehensility, 43

radial nerve, *45*
Raynaud's syndrome, 51–52
Redford, Robert, 57
reflex actions, 46
rheumatoid arthritis, 52–53
ring finger, *15,* 16, 42, 43
ring sign, 68, *68,* 69
rubella, 19
Ruth, Babe, 57

saddle joint, *37,* 38
scaphoid, *36*
scar, 33
Schirra, Wally, 57
scissors grip, 44, *44*
sebaceous gland, 24, *29*
sensory nerves, 45
sensory strips, *47,* 48
sign language, 66, 71–76
signing, 73, *74, 75,* 75–76
simian crease, *18,* 19
six-fingered hand, 15
skin, 17–29
skin senses, 35–39

spinal cord, 45, 46, 49
Spitz, Mark, 57
squirrel, 7, *7*
Stone Age tools, 60, *60*
subcutaneous tissue, *22,* 32
suntan, 23
sweat gland, *22,* 24
sweat pores, 21, *22,* 24
sweaty hands, 24, 34
syndactyly, 15, *15*
synovial joint, *37*

temperature (sense), 26, 28
tendon, 38
thumb, 7, 11, *15,* 16, 32, 37, 38,
  42, 43
  bones of, *36*
  opposable, 8
  size of, 17
thumbing a ride, 69
thumbing one's nose, 68, *68*
"thumbs up" sign, *68,* 69
tools, 9, 60, 61
touch (sense), 26, 27, 29
trapezium, *36*
trapezoid, *36*
trembling hands, 34
triquetral, *36*
Twain, Mark, 56

ulnar nerve, *45*

"V for victory" sign, *68,* 69, 70
veins, 50, *50,* 51

wart, 33–34
Washoe, 76
waving, 67, *67*
whorl, 20, *20*